555

Ways to Put More
Fun in Your Life

by Bob Basso, Ph.D.

The
Globe
Pequot
Press

Old Saybrook, Connecticut

Text design by Saralyn D'Amato

Library of Congress Cataloging-in-Publication Data

Basso, Bob.
    555 ways to put more fun in your life / by Bob Basso. — 1st ed.
      p. cm.
    ISBN 1-56440-385-8
    1. American wit and humor. I. Title. II. Title: Five hundred and fifty-five ways to put more fun in your life
    PN6162.B32   1994
818' .5402—dc20   94-15457
                                                     CIP

Manufactured in the United States of America
First Edition/First Printing

INTRODUCTION

I wrote this book because John Henry Di Giamo told me to put my money where my mouth was or forfeit my title of "America's number one fun motivator" bestowed on me by *People* magazine.

You see, I was tooling around the country in my "Funmobile," publicizing my book *This Job Should Be Fun* and stopping off in hospitals to speak to patients about the healing power of humor.

John Henry listened with his fellow patients in Dallas and then jumped up and playfully challenged me. "Everybody knows fun makes you feel good. You're not telling us anything new. Tell us how. *How* do you find the fun when half of your organs are on the fritz, you got a tube up your nose, and your rear end is always hanging out this damn hospital gown? What's the first step?"

I told him what my Dad, the fire chief, had told me when I was four and the most frightening monsters in the universe were popping up all over—in the closets, in dark corners, in the basement, and at night after Mom turned out the light and walked a few million miles away from me to her room. He said, "Laugh at your monsters. The longer you do, the smaller they get." That's the first step.

John Henry and his friends were quick learners. They began a wild, marvelously irreverent take-off on a chic fashion show displaying the latest haute couture in surgical dressings, body burn wraps, and petite and "big boy" catheters, fully accessorized with bedpans, wheelchairs, and the like. There was ward-shaking laughter and, I like to think, some instant healing going on.

When it died down, John Henry deadpanned. "So, what's the next step?"

I said, "There're a thousand and one things more you can do to start the fun rolling."

"Prove it," he said.

Okay, John, here's the first installment: 555 ways. I hope the suggestions on these pages bring you fun and a whole lot more. I hope they add zest, glitter, and a colorful path transforming boredom into play, tragedy into comedy, stillness into laughter, and, yes, pain into health and balance.

These thoughts are not all mine. Many were gleaned from a gaggle of sunshine warriors along my way—from presidents and clowns, cancer patients and super athletes, hobos, and a lot of relatives from my mother's side of the family—all accentuators of the positive, eliminators of the negative.

Try them all or try a few or create your own. But please, do try.

Have fun with your life. The alternative doesn't make any sense.

1

Put a red line through the name of every negative person in your address book.
Avoid these people.

2

Freeze in your mind the most stressful moment of your day. Now see it as a cartoon. Exaggerate it.
Laugh at the absurdity.

3

Declare "Be Good to Me" day. Tell the people around you to please observe this holiday.

4

Pretend you're a serious opera singer rehearsing a scene. Make a list of ten things that bug you about you. Stand before a mirror and "sing" each character flaw with wild, dramatic gestures. End with an epic death scene.

5

Floss your teeth to Tschaikovsky's 1812 Overture (with cannon).

6

Leave a thank-you note for your mailman.

7

Ask people what makes them laugh.
You'll both be howling in no time.

8

Picture a rainbow over the head of
everybody who gives you a tough time.
Next time they do, look at it.

9

Go to a senior citizens' dance.
Ask someone sturdy to jitterbug.

10

Make an audio tape of every positive,
life-affirming song you know. Keep it handy.

11

Sit in a bubble bath.
Sing "I'm in the Mood for Love."

12

Declare yourself a T.V. addict in rehabilitation.
Your self-prescribed therapy: Place a stack of
books on the T.V. set. Every time you feel the
urge to turn it on, grab a book and read.

13

Send a collect Strip O' Gram to a friendly rival. Include a note: "Let's cut out the window dressing and get down to the bare essentials on this matter. Whadayasay?"

14

Send yourself a Strip O' Gram. Make sure you have a room full of friends over at the time.

15

Dress up like the person you imagine yourself to be. Go somewhere. Act like that person.

16

Learn to say good morning in seven different languages. Start with Hindi: "Suprâbhatum."

17

Draw your dragon—a cartoon of the person who gives you the most hassles in life. Keep it handy when he or she starts breathing fire.

18

Put love notes in your mate's purse, pockets, or lunch pail.

19

Form a WAC (Wild and Crazy) club with two other zanies. Plan bizarre outings once a month; for example, go bowling in formal wear, organize a kazoo marching band for local parades, etc.

20

Talk to God as if He/She were your next-door neighbor.

21

Get in the habit of saying "It's not that important."

22

Create a "pity pot." Write your troubles down and throw them into the pot. At the end of the day, dump it in the trash can with a great big smile.

23

Join a beginner's comedy class in improvisation, standup, or writing. Check the local college extension programs for listings.

24

Write your own daily horoscope.

25

Pat yourself on the back when someone else should but doesn't.

26

Plan surprise dates with your mate. One tells the other to meet at a certain place at a prescribed time, and off you go on an adventure.

27

Hum all day. Humming tells the rest of your body everything's just fine.

28

Call your answering machine. Tell yourself what a fabulous person you are.

29

Take a hot bath with a rubber duck. Exchange life philosophies.

30

Spend one whole day taking nothing for granted. Look at everything in wonderment—starting your car, putting on your socks, watching birds in flight, listening to your mother-in-law—and say, "Isn't that really amazing."

31

Go out of your way to find something to congratulate someone for. Give the person an enthusiastic "high five."

32

Buy a ventriloquist's dummy. Make him your shrink. When you're in need of advice, talk it out with him. You'll be surprised just how wise those dummies are.

33

Hire a butler or French maid for a day.

34

Buy a kid's lunch box. Fill it the way your mother used to when you were younger. Bring it to work. Eat and enjoy.

35

Next time you get an annoying automated phone message, wait for the beep, then order a large pizza with 17 toppings.

36

Get up a half hour earlier in the morning. Read something by Woody Allen.

37

Put out your finest china and silverware. Have peanut butter and jelly sandwiches. Serve Kool Aid in wine glasses. Invite a friend over. Talk about what a good life you really have.

38

Hold TGIM (Thank God It's Monday) parties.

39

Learn exactly why the twelve o'clock digital readout keeps flashing on your VCR. Tell someone else.

40

Call time-out in the middle of trouble. Close your eyes. Do nothing. Something good will happen.

41

Turn in all your credit cards.

42

Memorize something Groucho Marx said. You might start with "Look for the absurdity in everything. You'll find it."

43

**Test drive a Mercedes Benz and
a Lamborghini in the same day.**

44

**Be Pollyanna for a day. Assume everybody you
meet today is out to do you good.**

45

Talk to the objects you buy.

46

Keep a baby picture of yourself in your wallet.
When things get bad, take it out and look at it.
Now, how bad can things be, hmnn?

47

Paint one wall of your home a different color
from the rest.

48

Befriend a weirdo.

49

"Stop taking yourself so seriously. You're not that important. After all, when you die, the size of your funeral will depend on the weather."
—Janet F. Basso (the author's mother)

50

Declare yourself a "gloom buster." Either lighten up the situation or walk away.

51

Fill your tub with Jell-O. The next step is up to your imagination.

52

Consider yourself a stand-up comedian in training. See everything you do as material for your routines.

53

Answer the phone with a super cheery hello. Changing your chemistry from negative to positive on the phone is the most effective way to take charge of the conversation.

54

Hire a clown to appear at the local children's hospital. Dress as his helper. Go with him.

55

**Spray your underpants
with expensive cologne.**

56

**Make a list of silly things people do, for
example, act guilty when they stand in the
"Ten Items or Less" check-out line with
more than ten items.**

57

Walk barefoot in the grass.

58

Have a candlelight dinner in the park at night.

59

Don't get out of bed until you've made one positive affirmation for your day.

60

Surprise yourself. Do something right now you wouldn't ordinarily do. For example, spend an hour in a flotation tank.

61

Erase the word *problem* from your vocabulary. Use *challenge*.

62

Slow down.

63

Clean the slate on personal conflicts. Approach all enemies and say, "Let's let bygones be bygones. Whadayasay?" Shake hands.

64

Send yourself a dozen roses.

65

Take a shower with a friend, fully clothed.

66

Call the public relations department of a major airline (preferably one in which you're enrolled as a frequent flyer). Ask them if you can take a ride in their flight simulator trainer.

67

Hold a wine and cheese "How to Program Your VCR" party.

68

Volunteer to help put up the circus next time it comes to town.

69

Give yourself a pet name, for example, Grand Slam Sammy, Racy Raul, Diana Dynamite.

70

Go to a psychic. Stop in the middle of the
session and read her fortune.

71

Put confetti in the letters you send to fun people.

72

Wink a little.

73

Talk to senior citizens every chance you get.

74

Take a risk.

75

**Write the White House. Ask for an invitation to
a state dinner. Don't be surprised if you get one.**

76

**When you're acting like a jerk, let the people
around you know *you* know. Stop and make
fun of yourself: "There I go again, acting like
the second son of the Almighty"
(or something like that).**

77

Make a preposterous looking suggestion box.
(Put wings, a moustache, and a toupee on your
piggy bank.) Every day drop in a suggestion.
Make suggestions to improve every single thing
in your life. Read them at the end of the month.
It's the best advice you'll ever get.

78

Organize a bicycle safari. Go to the zoo.

79

Dress exactly the way you feel.

80

Learn to imitate celebrities. It's easy:

First, copy their gestures, characteristics, facial expressions.

Second, listen to the "music" (the rhythm) of their speech patterns. Hum that rhythm.

Third, put the characteristics and the humming together.

Fourth, drop the humming and try talking like them.

Voilà! A genuine impersonation.

81

Wear spats.

82

Skip down the street. (When you were a kid, things always got better when you skipped. It's a mystery, but it's so.)

83

Write to Yassir Arafat. Suggest he get a shave and haircut. Give him the name of a good tailor.

84

Do a five-minute comedy roast of yourself before a mirror.

85

Pick the starriest night of the year.
Climb a hill. Lie on your back and look at
every star above you. Sigh a lot.

86

Get in the habit of saying "Thank you, God, for
another day. I'm going to make it count."

87

Rainy day déjà vu: Do your best imitation of
Gene Kelly's famous song and dance number in
Singin' in the Rain.

88

Start a Wacky Word Club. Pick a fun partner at work. Every day each of you brings in a fun word for the other to define. Examples: spelunker, gemutlichkeit, jock-eyed, etc. Keep score of correct answers. At the end of the month, the loser has to spring for two tickets to a fun event.

89

Ask little kids, "What's the meaning of life?" Listen to the answers.

90

Change the way you strut your stuff. Try a new walk one day, a different posture the next, etc.

91

Invent a new pizza with the wildest toppings imaginable.

92

Keep a "What's Funny about Me" log. Make at least three entries a day.

93

Have a picnic in the most unusual place you can imagine, for example, a walk-in toy closet, the middle of a football stadium (off season, of course), the rumble seat of a '28 Chevy.

94

Personalize every piece of machinery in your environment. For example, the vacuum cleaner becomes "Big Bertha," the blender becomes "Crazy Harry."

95

Play on a jungle gym late at night.

96

Make believe you are a candid camera. Turn yourself on several times a day. Find people doing funny and offbeat things when they don't suspect you're watching. Watch your serious notions of life change rapidly.

97

Cut out every negative bit of news from the morning paper. Show what's left to someone else. Draw your own conclusions.

98

Dance naked under a full moon.

99

Imitate every bizarre person you meet. Store them in your "living characters" memory file. Bring them out occasionally.

100

Start a "first timer's" club. Seek experiences you've never had before. For example, go to a square dance, run the rapids, gate crash a Greek wedding (bring a gift), etc.

101

Referee a kids' sporting event.

102

Go to a nudist beach. Wear a fig leaf
(or leaves) for starters.

103

Create your alter ego—the person who always
wins. Dress the way that character would dress
and go somewhere and win. (Suggestion: Don't
make Las Vegas your first stop.)

104

Forgive somebody for past transgressions.

105

Fax a cartoon to a sourpuss.

106

Be inconsistent. Set your table with your best china and then use an old sneaker as your centerpiece. Enjoy the irony.

107

Come up with a new philosophy of life every day. Attach it to the dashboard of your car. Talk to yourself about it on the way to work.

108

Learn to tango.

109

Brush your teeth pretending to be a different celebrity every morning. Interview yourself.

110

Sleep in a pup tent in your living room. You'll wake up with a different perspective of the world.

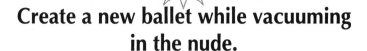

111

Create a new ballet while vacuuming
in the nude.

112

Make believe you're posing for a *Playboy*
or *Playgirl* centerfold. Don't let your
mother catch you.

113

Ask yourself, "Am I doing what I love to do? If
not, why not?" Pay attention to the answer.

114

Put a red light in your refrigerator.

115

As soon as you open your eyes in the morning, shout out, "I will not entertain a negative thought today!" And don't.

116

Call someone for no other reason than to say what a great person he or she is.

117

Rub peppermint oil on your body.
Sit in a hot tub.

118

Make a date with someone to go
on a sunrise hike.

119

Hug a tree.

120

Declare one day a year "Makeover Day." Observe it. Change everything about you that you can: hair, socks, underwear, odor, attitude, eating habits, schedules, friends—the whole works.

121

Dress sleazy. Walk around the block.
Get it out of your system.

122

Ride in the back seat of your own car— but not while driving, please.

123

Celebrate another religion's high holy days. Do it sincerely and watch your understanding grow. That's always fun.

124

Take a ride on a merry-go-round.

125

Buy a fake car phone. Talk to all the "movers and shakers" in your life. Tell them what you *really* think.

126

Wear wild and crazy underwear to your annual physical.

127

Pick a provocative question. Take a survey.

128

Make a list titled "Advice My Mother Always Gave Me."

129

Choose the "Child's Play" art
for your designer checks.

130

Give your Christmas gifts at Thanksgiving.

131

Invite Dr. Ruth to lunch.

132

Go to a Mexican film festival.

133

Make your own underwear!

134

**Fellas, get a crew cut.
Ladies, get a fifties-type hairstyle.**

135

**Tell your doctor to make you laugh
before he or she works on you.**

136

**Get yourself a little blue security blanket like
Linus in the "Peanuts" comic strip.**

137

Take a nun to lunch.

138

**Help start a "laughter room" at a local hospital
(a room set aside where patients and visitors
can watch comedy videos, read humor magazines,
and listen to funny audio tapes).
Humor is the best medicine.**

139

Take a ride in a seaplane.

140

Browse in old book stores.

141

Wash your car in the rain.

142

Take a moonlight horseback ride.

143

Play Santa Claus.

144

Go to baseball spring training games in Arizona or Florida. It's the way baseball was meant to be played—for fun, close to the fans, and very loose. (For a spring training schedule, write Office of Commissioner, Major League Baseball, 350 Park Avenue, New York, NY 10022.)

145

Drive a convertible. Wear goggles, a scarf, and an old aviator's hat.

146

Chew bubble gum on the way to work.

147

Look for paradise on earth. Send away
for brochures, watch travelogues, ask world
travelers. Find a way to get there.

148

At the turnpike toll booth, pay for
the car behind you.

149

Smile and say hello to five strangers a day.

150

Keep a "good stuff only" diary. Realize now what you surely will realize later—that only the good stuff really matters.

151

Climb a tree. Do your Tarzan yell. (Make sure there're no elephants in the area.)

152

Buy a little beanie with a propeller on top. Make it your thinking cap. Use it often.

153

Travel Cheaply. Try hosteling—staying at discounted inns and hotels that provide dormitory-style living quarters for younger travelers. Many of them stretch the definition of young to include any biped that's breathing. (Write American Youth Hostels, Dept. 855, P.O. Box 37613, Washington, D.C. 20013, or call 202–783–6161.)

154

Call one of your old schoolteachers
just to say hi.

155

Get a foot massage.

156

Give a foot massage.

157

Take a mini vacation every week. Walk in the park, eat popcorn, visit a museum.

158

Plan a hoax with a friend.

159

Order something from the Frederick's of Hollywood catalogue.

160

Buy a comic book. Read it before an important meeting.

161

Hold a "lipsync" party.

162

Get an artist to do a caricature of you.

163

Wear corduroy pants.

164

Throw out half the paperwork in your house.

165

Send your Christmas cards in June.

166

Plan to visit every amusement park in America.

167

**Buy a Flexi-flyer sled.
Go belly-whopping in the snow.**

168

Go to a pet store. Play with a puppy.
Buy the puppy. Give it to a shut-in person you
know who really needs it.

169

Listen to the Grand Ole Opry on radio.

170

Rename all your enemies with the names of
comic book characters.

171

Dunk some Oreos in milk. Eat them very slowly.

172

Catch snowflakes on your tongue.

173

Give your computer an affectionate user-friendly name. "Sunshine," "Love child," "Big Bopper" are all nice.

174

Talk to your favorite departed historical character. Chat about things. Ask for advice. Listen. (Ben Franklin and Eleanor Roosevelt are particularly responsive.)

175

Try staying in a college dorm on your next vacation. More than 650 colleges and universities in the U.S., Canada, and Europe open their dormitories to travelers every summer. (For information and a directory, write Campus Travel Service, P.O. Box 5007, Laguna Beach, CA 92652, or call 714–497–3044.)

176

Get a weekend job at an amusement park.

177

Hold a liars' contest.

178

Start a great conversationalists' club. Preset the topic. Everybody does research on it. Get together and chat. Only rule: When you open your mouth, you have to contribute new information.

179

Write a fan letter to yourself. Answer it.

180

Drive through New England in the fall.

181

Keep a hand puppet. Call it your whipping boy/girl. Next time you have the urge to tell someone off, try it first on the puppet. Chances are, that's as far as it'll go.

182

Get in the pit with a mud wrestler. Tickle a lot.

183

Go body surfing in the buff.

184

Start off every meeting by asking for a joke.

185

Fill your shorts with Cool Whip.

186

Make a sick person laugh.

187

Spend Saturday morning in the library.

188

**Call the cancer ward of your local hospital.
Ask the duty nurse for the name of a patient she
thinks would enjoy a giant balloon bouquet.
Send it.**

189

Visit your old neighborhood. Play one of the games you used to play when you were a kid.

190

Run for president.

191

Paint on a facial beauty mark. Change its position every day.

192

Bake the world's most unusual-looking cookies.

193

Hold a "Wackiest Person I Ever Met" costume party. Dress and act like your person of choice.

194

Figure out the funniest last words you could say before making your final exit from this crazy world. Remember them—for later.

195

Spend a night in a ghost town.

196

Wear an eye patch. Make up a silly excuse to give to folks who want to know why, for example, "I'm in my Captain Hook phase."

197

Take a group of senior citizens to a pinball joint or an arcade. Play the games. You pick up the tab.

198

Plan a "This Is Your Life" surprise party for a friend. Arrange to have childhood friends, teachers, relatives, and significant VIPs make an appearance. Write a script. Accentuate the positive.

199

Realize most people you meet work very, very hard at making life much more serious than it was ever intended to be. Be gentle with them, but don't be impressed by them.

200

**Visit a lighthouse. Listen for the sounds
of its history.**

201

**Change your refrigerator door magnets every
month.**

202

**Send one of those twelve-foot novelty telegrams
to a friend who needs cheering up.**

203

Pick the one hobby in the world you would most enjoy. Approach it with wild enthusiasm.
Become an expert.

204

Go to bed before nine o'clock.

205

Ask for a round of applause.

206

Create your own personal superhero. Costume yourself as him or her. Take a picture. When evil lurks around you, look at that picture and know you have a personal champion who will always come to the rescue.

207

Wanna meet fun people? Wear a Halloween mask to the supermarket.

208

Soak your face in ice water.

209

Leave ego-building messages for yourself on the fridge.

210

Put on a classical recording. Conduct the orchestra. Get into it. Go bananas.

211

Visit an elephant. Tell him or her a "knock-knock" joke.

212

Send Thanksgiving cards. Personalize them by saying thank-you for a particular kindness.

213

Keep a scrapbook of the best jokes you've ever heard. One day you'll be asked to speak in front of an audience. Picking the right jokes makes a good speech better—much better.

214

Wear argyle socks.

215

Deliver a dozen pizzas to a neighborhood orphanage.

216

Try out for a community theater musical. If you don't get the part, volunteer to work backstage.

217

Use silk pillow cases.

218

Congratulate everybody who wins at something.

219

Write a mini-musical comedy of your life. What song titles would you include? Sing them to somebody.

220

Quote your mother often.

221

Wear polka dots.

222

**Take a self-assertion course.
Wear your most colorful outfit.**

223

**Do a wild, sensuous strip tease for an
imaginary audience. (Make sure your front
door is locked.)**

224

Learn to do the Texas two-step.

225

Copy cartoons on your stationery.

226

Play the kazoo.

227

Paint each toenail a different color.

228

Wear a different perfume or after-shave scent every day.

229

Have a beach party in your living room on the coldest day of the year.

230

Order something furry from the L.L. Bean catalogue.

231

Ask everybody you meet, "What's the most fun, off-beat thing you do?"

232

Put a feather in your shorts. Think about it from time to time.

233

Cut down on your expenses. Copy a picture of your mother and put it on all your credit cards. Next time you get the urge to spend, look at mother. What would she say, hmnnn?

234

Keep a glob of silly putty handy.

235

Seek out your childhood heros or heroines.
Tell them how much you admired them.
If they're not around anymore, write to
their relatives.

236

Get all your Christmas shopping done by
September 1.

237

Memorize a quotation that advocates finding fun in life. Example: "Nothing, no experience good or bad, no cause is in itself momentous enough to monopolize the whole of life to the exclusion of laughter." —Alfred North Whitehead

238

Rent a houseboat for a day.

239

Write your children a fan letter.

240
Go to a magic store. Buy a trick.

241
Ride a tricycle.

242
Change the interior colors of at least one room
in your home every year.

243
Buy something homemade in a country store.

244

Keep an "idea book" with you at all times. Whenever you get an idea for a new product, think of a better way to do something, create a new game show, or come up with a novel excuse for staying home from work, write it down.

245

Look for funky, off-beat shops everywhere you go. Stop in and browse.

246

Pay all your bills as soon as you receive them.

247

Make a "Coming Attractions" bulletin board. Visualize all the upcoming color, fun, and excitement you want in your life, for example, a dream vacation in Sri Lanka, IRS refund, hot date, zero body fat. Then cut out pictures and graphics that represent them. Funny, but when you visualize the things you want, you usually get them.

248

Let someone lead you astray.
(Make it a short, harmless trip.)

249

Call the Home Shopping Network. Make them
an offer on the host's pants.

250

Simplify. Get rid of things. Once a month,
donate 10 percent of your wardrobe or garage
storage to charity.

251

Keep asking yourself in everything you do, How can I enjoy this?

252

Uncover your family history before the turn of the century. Write the Church of Latter-Day Saints Family History Library, c/o Correspondence, 35 North West Temple, Salt Lake City, UT 84150, or call (801) 240–1000 ext. 2364.

253

Make your bedroom a theme park—
jungle safari, Old West, the Land of Oz—and
give it a wild and crazy name.

254

Leave a thank-you balloon for the
garbage collectors.

255

Write an anonymous letter to the most difficult
person in your life. Say what a swell person he
or she is. (Little things mean a lot.)

256

Give yourself a facial.

257

Find the room, closet, garage, shower, or other space where you are most creative. Dub it your "think tank." Bring your problems there often.

258

Say thank you every time you're criticized.

259

Wear a Mickey Mouse pinky ring.

260

Got a problem at work? Forget about
calling a meeting; call for a "two-minute drill."
Huddle and shoot ideas at one another
with a two-minute limit. Solutions only—
no griping, no speechmaking—only positive
ideas. Making problem solving a game
is the most effective way to
unleash creativity.

Don't join clubs, start them.

Start a morning walking club.

Become famous for your short business meetings.

264

If you don't understand a problem, explain it to a group of people and listen to yourself. Ask questions. Invariably, the answer will appear.

265

Go to a punk rock concert. Costume yourself appropriately. Talk hip: for example, "dude," "boss," "fer sure," "rad," etc.

266

Put a canopy over your bed.

267

Entertain the idea of completely changing your living environment. Call several reputable real estate agents in the area in which you want to live. Ask them to look for a creative space such as an old firehouse, a deserted country store, an artist's loft, a tug boat. Check them out.

268

Learn to say yes to good ideas and no to garbage. Smile either way. Make no excuses for your decisions.

269

Spend a morning in an elementary schoolroom. You'll regain a wholesome perspective on life very quickly.

270

Read the issue of your hometown newspaper that was published on the date you were born.

271

Put a child's cartoon-theme comforter on your bed. Peanuts is fun. So are Mickey and Donald.

272

Surround yourself with plants.

273

Memorize, with a friend, Abbott and Costello's classic routine, "Who's On First?" Do it every chance you get.

274

Put a sidecar on your bicycle.
Take a friend for a ride.

275

Read the encyclopedia from A to Z.
Jot down provocative or little-known facts.
Work them into your daily conversation, for
example: "Did you know that dueling is legal
in Uruguay, as long as both parties are
registered blood donors?"

276

Track down a childhood friend.
Have lunch together.

277

Smile at a rabbi.

278

Wear your old high school sweatshirt.

279

When writing a business memo, add fun descriptive phrases after the person's name, for example: "To Edith, role model and homecoming queen" or "To Arnold, a Rocky Marciano look-alike."

280

Make a six-foot blowup of the wackiest photo of you.

281

Make a deal with your friends and
family: no store-bought gifts this Christmas, only
presents you've personally hand made. If you're
not handy, write a poem and frame it.

282

Dab your personal letters with your cologne.

283

Go to your high school's homecoming game.

284

Pass out balloons in a doctor's office.

285

Kibitz with God.

286

Never pass a nurse without telling her what a great job she's doing.

287

Giggle for no reason at all.

288

Listen to old folks talking. Ask their advice on something. Whatever they tell you will be useful.

289

Become an expert on sex. Share your knowledge.

290

Record your own eulogy. Talk only about your upbeat, funny side. (It's the only side people want to remember, anyway.) Put in your will that it is the only one to be given.

291

Go on a self-improvement binge. Attend a workshop, seminar, or course you think will make you better informed.

292

Pose before a mirror as if you were Mr./Ms. Universe.

293

Never pass by a toy store without dropping in.

294

**Become a connoisseur of something good
to eat or drink—lichee nuts, wine,
Pop Tarts—anything.**

295

**Call the IRS and tell them they're
doing a great job.**

296

**Figure out what animal the
people around you look like.**

297

Assess your energy level at any given time as a position on an automobile's gear shift. If your "power train" feels weak, physically shift your imaginary stick shift into second, third, or overdrive. Silly? You bet. But it works. You're sending a visual image to your brain of what you want, and you'll get it!

298

Make love in a closet.

299

Soak your feet in warm, sudsy water.

300

Read children's books.

301

Become an advocate for something.

302

Climb a small mountain.

303

Put up a "Wacky News" bulletin board. Paste up funny headlines, malapropisms, or unintended humor from any printed source. (Example from a corporate employee's guide to earthquake survival: "In case of an earthquake, get under your desk and cooperate with your supervisor.")

304

Beat gridlock. Make your car a mobile classroom. Forget the radio. Play comedy and self-help tapes everywhere you go.

305

Be extremely enthusiastic first thing in the morning. It sets your tone for the rest of the day.

306

Acknowledge every kindness with a thank-you note.

307

Ask your body how it's doing. Listen. It'll give you an answer.

308

Create a stress megaphone. Make it colorful (the wackier, the better). When stress strikes, pick it up and announce, "Stress attack! Help! I need a laugh real quick." Watch the people around you happily rally to the cause.

309

Devise your own mental healing process. For example, visualize firemen with their hoses dousing the pain with healing water.

310

Declare "Music Appreciation Day."
Play the works of one master all day long.
Another day pick another master.
Soon you'll appreciate them all.

311

Design your own greeting cards
from recycled paper.

312

Invite someone to dinner and
go dressed as clowns.

313

Take a belly dancing course.

314

Cut out the dialogue below
cartoons. Write your own.

315

Put zebra-striped seat covers in your car.

316

Become a backtrails bicyclist.

317

Discover something new
about your neighborhood.

318

Go bananas at an amusement arcade.
Play everything that looks fun.

319

Hit yourself in the face with a pie.
Have an audience handy.

320

Make a "Count Your Blessings Scoreboard."
Every morning list one happy, positive thing that
makes your life good.

321

Write down your "Rules of Life."
Add to them frequently.

322

Smuggle your own snacks into
the movies.

323

Make up a coupon book of fabulous fun adventures (with pictures). For example, "Cocktails, candlelight, and a first night at the theater"; "Shoot the rapids"; "Champagne in a hot-air balloon." After a significant personal achievement, tear one out and treat yourself. You deserve it.

324

Before you go to sleep, visualize the dream you want to have.

325

Every day learn two different words in a foreign language.

326

Search for the funniest toy you can find. Bring it home and play with it.

327

Write out a list of the funniest things that have happened to you in your life. Prominently display it. Add to it frequently.

328

Send in plot ideas to the producers of your favorite sitcoms.

329

If you're thinking of buying a foreign car, do it on your next European vacation. Many dealers will fly you free from your port of entry to the factory. It's lots cheaper, too. That's fun.

330

Burst out in song for no reason at all.

331

Give only humorous novelty gifts for presents, for example, a laughing mirror, a designer doll bearing the recipient's face, a year's supply of fortune cookies.

332

Know someone with low self-esteem? Find something to compliment them on. Do it often.

333

Organize every closet in your home.

334

Go to opening night at the opera. Wear the "Phantom's mask" with cape.

335

Send a "CARE package" to a person in the service.

336

Get fifteen people together for a cruise. You go free. Contact your local travel agent for details.

337

Research the development of humor down through the ages.

338

Listen for hunches. Follow one to its conclusion.

339

Become a history buff. Pick an event, personality, or era and read everything you can on the subject. Volunteer to speak on it at a local civic club.

340

Learn the rebel yell.

341

Drive to the country. Buy fresh vegetables.

342

Declare one day a month "Off-the-Wall Day" with your spouse. Alternate planning something bizarre to do together; for example, go grocery shopping in formal wear or attend a lecture on Estonian poetry.

343

Stay at a motel by the sea. Keep the windows open. Fall asleep to the sound of the waves.

344

Pretend you have laryngitis. Spend a whole day listening to what people are saying. Silly, ain't it?

345

Be illogical all day.

346

Wear a new article of clothing with the sales tag still attached. See how long it takes people to tell you. Then say, "Yes, I know, but thank you." Then go about your business.

347

Turn off the sound on the evening newscast. Play classical music as you watch the day's madness unfold. (Keeps everything in perspective.)

348

Start believing that life is a process, not a result.

349

Play mud football.

350

Declare personal holidays, for example, Computer Literacy Day, commemorating the day you learned to operate your computer sans manual.

351

Invite all the wackiest people you know to dinner. Invite the "squarest" person you know to join you.

352

Try this conversation starter: Customize a T-shirt to say "Hi, I'm from (name of your hometown). Where are you from?"

353

String a hammock between two trees in the woods.

354

Hold a "Healthy B.Y.O.F." party. Everybody brings an unusual, tasty, healthy dish.

355

Pretend you understand modern art.

356

Adopt grandparents.

357

**Research and find the healthiest, most
inexpensive town in America to live. Visit it.
Think about moving. (Read the September issue
of *Money* magazine, which contains a
"Best Places to Live" survey.)**

358

Sing all your worries as if they were love songs.

359

Interview people who make money doing
the thing they love to do. Find out how they
made the big decision to go after their dream.
Think about it.

360

Moon yourself in a mirror.

361

Say howdy instead of hello.

362

Laugh at people who cut you off
on the freeway.

363

Volunteer at your local humane society. Talk to
the animals.

364

Call someone and ask for a joke.

365

Fun starts when you put your life in balance. Nothing works very well until you do. Write down what you need in work, play, and love to put you on an even keel. Smile—you're already on your way.

366

Always be in training for something.

367

Determine the best thing you do. Teach a course in it.

368

Declare "Hooray for Spontaneity Day":
Listen to that inner voice and do everything,
go anywhere the voice directs you.
Experience complete freedom.

369

Buy an extra Christmas tree. Leave it at
a stranger's door with a note:
"There *is* a Santa Claus."

370

Give everybody a big cheery greeting
when you step on an elevator.

371

Volunteer to work on a bowl game parade float.

372

On hot days, put your underwear in the refrigerator for a half hour before going out.

373

Lie naked on a sheepskin rug before a roaring fire.

374

Shadow box with your nemesis. Win by a TKO.

375

Learn to be a stand-up comedian. Start by talking about all those little things people do that tick you off and then comment about them. For example, "Why do people always look into their handkerchief after they blow their nose? What do they expect to find? 'Hey, hey, there's that old running shoe I've been looking for.'"

376

Find a cheaper way to do everything.

377

Organize a comedy roast for a friend.

378

Make a list of all the things you loved to do as a kid. Start doing them again.

379

Challenge a kid to a spelling bee.

380

Tell yourself a bedtime story.

381

Learn the names of wildflowers.

382

Bring your own music to your next dentist's appointment. Play it. (If he won't let you, get a new dentist.)

383

Traffic come to a standstill? Get out of the car and do your best Ethel Merman imitation of "Everything's Coming Up Roses."

384

Make your morning grooming ritual a ballet.

385

Replace your front door bell with a novelty sound such as "Ding dong, the witch is dead," reveille bugle call, the mating call of the gooney bird, etc.

386

Buy a laughter cassette. Play it first thing in the morning.

387

Wish upon a star.

388

Eat baby food.

389

Get an introduction to any guy named Rocco.

390

Paint the inside of your garage bright colors.

391

Become an expert on something obscure, for instance, the films of Sonny Tufts, the hand gestures of the Queen of England, undergarments of Colonial America. Lecture on it.

392

Stand at the top of a mountain, spread your arms, and shout at the top of your voice with as much gusto as possible, "Let Go!" See all your negative thinking fly away.

393

Wear a safari outfit. Go to the zoo.
Take pictures of you and the animals.

394

Book passage to anywhere on a freighter.
(For information, call Freighter World,
818–449–3106, and request a list
of freighter lines.)

395

Visit a shut-in. Bring ice cream, big
cookies, and a Benny Hill video.

396

Let a kid show you how to do "new math."

397

Keep a fantasy diary. Make imaginary entries of the things you'd like to happen; for example: "Beat Martina in four straight sets this morning. Told boss I'm worth twice my salary. Canceled my appointment with the orthodontist. Chartered a jet to Spain; ran with the bulls at Pamplona."

398

Buy the Boy Scout or Girl Scout Handbook. Practice some of the outdoor skills taught, for instance, boxing the compass, starting a fire, identifying types of trees, avoiding poison ivy.

399

Be open to all knowledge. Check the "Things to Do" section of your newspaper's weekend edition. Attend what for you would be the most outrageous free community lecture— "How to Make Friends with a Donkey," " Learn to Love Your Feet," " How to Hold a Jell-O Cook-off," etc.

400

Put on your favorite background music. Fingerpaint your masterpiece. (Silly? Sure, but some of the most well-recognized pieces of modern art started out the same way.)

401

Wear a loin cloth. Walk in the woods. (Don't forget your mosquito repellent.)

402

Surprise a friend. Arrange for a mud bath for two.

403

Start breaking your fear barriers. List all the
adventurous activities that scare the bejaybers
out of you, for instance, parasailing, water-skiing,
dating much younger people, etc.
Learn the rules and just do it.

404

Invite over a few of your friends. Put on one of
those ridiculous sci-fi movies. Turn off the sound.
Make up your own dialogue.

405

Eat dessert first.

406

Play all the songs recorded by Spike Jones and his orchestra.

407

Check all the pictures and decorations adorning your walls. If they're not bright, cheery, and uplifting, replace them, pronto.

408

Start a fan club for the most positive person you know.

409

Make reservations to attend the New Orleans Mardi Gras one year in advance. Call the chamber of commerce and find out how you can participate in the big parade.

410

Go on an appreciation binge. Write letters of appreciation to the bosses of the friendliest service people you deal with.

411

Seek out great storytellers. Listen and smile.

412

Become an obscure facts junkie. Sprinkle them into your conversations: "Did you know that many piranha are vegetarians? That Venezuelan cowboys ride barefooted, with spurs?" That kind of stuff.

413

Fall in love with colorful adjectives, for example, *rhapsodic, frothy, Dada-esque, neo-virtual, boustrophedon.* Write them down whenever you read or hear them. Sprinkle them into your conversations often.

414

Plan an "adventure" with a kid, something neither of you has done before, for instance, wait at a stage door to get a star's autograph, go to the library and find out why the monkeys in Zamboanga have no tails, etc.

415

Watch sumo wrestling on T.V.
Cheer for the lighter guy.

416

Go to a German Oktoberfest in your area.

417

Create your own personal awards—Most Polite, Always Prompt, Biggest Smile, Best Accessorized, etc. Award frequently.

418

Find a budding artist of any age. Encourage him or her mightily. Help the artist hold a one-person Sunday art show in the park—help carry the art, set it up, and make sure people know about it.

419

Sleep on the ground near a stream.

420

Become somebody's "king's fool" for a day.
Your job: Play harmless practical jokes, plan
surprises, color their day with anything positive
that makes them laugh.

421

Never sleep with someone whose
troubles are worse than yours.

422

Never sleep with someone who has
no sense of humor.

423

Shop at secondhand stores. Come up with a cheap but sharp-looking period outfit. Wear it.

424

Become a pen pal with someone from a country you always wanted to visit. One day you'll go there, and having a pal will make the experience doubly enriching. (For more information, send a self-addressed stamped envelope to International Pen Pals, P.O. Box 290065, Brooklyn, NY 11229–0001.)

425

Become a great storyteller.

Step #1 Close your eyes. Picture an interesting event in your life.

Step #2 "See" all the elements in your story—colors, characters, atmosphere, and sounds.

Step #3 Describe everything you see in vivid detail.

Step #4 Open your eyes. Now talk about the event that took place there.

Great storytellers paint living pictures. It's an acquired skill. Practice often.

426

Go on a gourmet coffee tasting spree.

427

Buy a one-person rubber boat.
Head it into the waves.

428

Establish a "Rites of Spring" tradition for the first day of spring. For example, donate lots of your possessions to charity; open a kid's lemonade stand; climb a small mountain, spread your arms and sing "Younger Than Springtime." Something that's uniquely yours.

429

Take your favorite poem to the middle of the woods. Read it to the trees. They'll love it.

430

Taste the ethnic foods of every country in the world.

431

Go to a centenarian's birthday party. Ask the honoree for his secrets of long life. Have your picture taken with him.
Don't forget what he said.

432

Spend a whole day going out of your way
to help people.

433

Talk somebody else into a bungee jump.

434

Pick the most beautiful climbable hill you can
find. Get to the top before dawn. Bring a
cassette player. As the day begins, play
"Morning" from the *Peer Gynt Suite*, by Grieg.

435

Read Will Rogers' quotes out loud.

436

Rent vacation videos from the most exotic spots in the world. Watch them while eating dinner.

437

Seek understanding, not agreement, in your communications. It will immediately improve your interpersonal skills and reduce your stress level a whole lot.

438

Sit down and let your libido fly. Start writing the raunchiest, most sensually explicit romance novel you can imagine. Don't think, just write trash. (After you've made your first million, please be kind and remember where you got the idea.)

439

Organize an ice skating party in August.

440

Go lawn bowling with some senior citizens.

441

Program kindness into everything you do.

442

Don't care who gets the credit.

443

Make a Roman toga from an old sheet. Wear it. Imagine you are one of the great orators from the Roman senate. Pick the issue on which you have the greatest passion and deliver it to an imaginary audience. (This is one of the most effective ways to improve your presentation skills.)

444

Sit on the bowsprit of a boat and take the ocean spray.

445

Stand under a waterfall.

446

Interview someone who claims to have been abducted by space aliens.

447

Don't wait until you're motivated.
Leap first.

448

Roll down a hillside into a pile of leaves.

449

Take your mother to the most expensive
restaurant in town. Fib—tell her you won
the dinner in a contest. It's the only way
she'll have any fun.

450

Have a T-shirt made with your personal philosophy written on the front.

451

Have someone pull you in a little red wagon.

452

Declare yourself an explorer today. Go where you've never been. Shout "Eureka!" a few times.

453

Tell someone they have a dynamite smile.

454

Spend a whole day asking for *exactly* what you want.

455

List all the places in your life where you're "stuck." Find the highest authority in each area. Call for help. Declare yourself "unstuck," because you are. Celebrate.

456

Put a six-foot stuffed figure of anything in your living room.

457

Be satisfied with small improvements in people and things.

458

Bring a flower to your favorite supermarket clerk.

459

Face the wind. Breathe deeply.

460

Create your own wild, energetic Latin American
dance. Simple. Turn on some appropriate music.
Close your eyes and let the rhythms move you.
Go with the impulse. Give it a spicy name—
"El Bombardo."

461

Erase all negative criticism of everybody.

462

Get rid of your bed. Buy a futon.

463

Spend Christmas on the Hawaiian island of Molokai with the friendliest, most caring folks you'll find in the South Pacific. No snow, but wagonsful of tradition and warmth.

464

Drive any car made in the thirties.

465

Assume you're not too old for anything. Take up
a kid's game. Try skate boarding.

466

Climb a sand dune. Play the score from
Lawrence of Arabia on a cassette.
Let your imagination take over.

467

Create a new fashion. Tear, rip, and reshape an
old set of clothes. Wear them.

468

Do a character study of the happiest person you know. Imitate him or her.

469

Hold a juice-tasting party. Everybody brings a personally blended concoction.

470

Play tourist in your own hometown. Take all the tours.

471

Get naked in the rain.

472

Sit on the beach during a blustery day.

473

Apply to be a contestant on your favorite game show.

474

Hold a "Favorite Passage" reading party.

475

Go fly a kite.

476

Attend a premier of anything.

477

As soon as you start to fear anything,
sit down and personalize it by drawing a
cartoon character of it. Everything's a cartoon:
life, death, and all the silly stuff in between.
So see those monsters for what they really are—
silly stick figures with no power to hurt if you
get the right perspective.

478

Call someone early in the morning just to wish them a great day.

479

Volunteer to help harvest grapes in a vineyard.
(Write Napa Valley Vintners Association,
P.O. Box 141, St. Helena, CA 94574,
or call 707–963–0148.)

480

Wear a Groucho nose and glasses
while driving to work.

481

Become an expert on the country you'd most like to visit.

482

Play music when you write a letter. It helps you find the right words.

483

Look at Magic Johnson's smile. Imitate it often.

484

Buy the wackiest alarm clock you can find.

485

Call a local celebrity. Tell her you want to interview her for the local newspaper. Do it and submit it. (Start with the fun people. They'll make it a breeze for you.)

486

Roller skate to church.

487
Think like a kid.

488

Rent *Ten from Your Show of Shows* from the comedy section of your video store. Invite friends over. See what humor used to be before the dirty words, putdowns, and obnoxious cynicism took over.

489
Creative problem solving: Write down at least twenty solutions to any problem you're facing. The best answer will be among your suggestions.

490

Pick your favorite person from history or folklore—Einstein, Amelia Earhart, ET, Sitting Bull, Louis "Satchmo" Armstrong, 007, Mae West, etc. Live one day the way you think that person would have lived it.

491

Give away your entire wardrobe. Start over. Be more colorful and innovative this time.

492

Eat only fruit for lunch.

493

Arrange to have someone serve you breakfast in bed. (See if you can also arrange to have them do the dishes afterward.)

494

Keep creativity alive: Frequently ask yourself, Is there a better way to do this? Just raising the question keeps you free of routine and open to additional possibilities.

495

Wear a turban.

496

For one whole day see everything in the human condition as absurdity.

497

Read the entire works of Mark Twain.

498

Play the "You're Not Going to Get My Goat" game during conflict. The more intense your adversary gets, the cooler you get, and the more mellow you smile.

499

Keep a scrapbook of unusual
vacation ideas.

500

Contact a local kindergarten teacher. Volunteer to
demonstrate one of your work skills or hobbies as
a show-and-tell session.

501

Be the first to enter an amusement park when it
opens in the morning.

502

Invite somebody going through a hard time to a
live comedy performance.

503

Say to your conscience, "What do you think?"
Listen. You'll always get an answer.

504

Every time tension mounts, press your nose
and make the sound of an old automobile
horn honking.

505

Go on a foreign movie kick.
See every one in town.

506

Buy "natural environments" cassettes—jungle
rain, morning in the woods, crashing waves, etc.
Play them before you go to sleep.

507

Take one-minute vacations every day. Close your
eyes. Visualize your dream spot. See yourself
exploring its joys and wonders.

508

Be imaginative. Write an incredibly positive
history of your life from this moment on.
Look at it. Make it happen. (It's the one
common strategy superachievers use to
get what they want. Give it a shot.)

509

Stop at an apple farm. Drink the juice of freshly
mashed apples.

510

Lie down in wet grass.

511

Have a spur-of-the-moment mini-reunion. Call a
dozen old school chums. Arrange to meet in the
ol' hangout joint from way back when.

512

When you go to another city, look up people
in the phone book with your last name.
Call them. See if there's a connection.

513

Give a speech in pantomime.

514

Go to a wine-tasting party. Act as if you know what you're doing. Ooh and aah a lot. Raise your eyebrows and say, "Hmmmnnn." Watch. Many will seek your counsel.

515

Read the comics section before you read the front page.

516

Next time the voice at the other end of the phone says, "May I ask who's calling?" say, "Yes."

517

Buy a dart board. Put the words "Negative Thoughts" across the face. When the buggers invade your thinking, call time-out. Start throwing.

518

Find silly substitutes for all the swear words you use, for example, "bull-dickey-boom-boom," "walla-walla-bing-bang," "ah-boffaloomby."

519

Fill your bedroom with balloons.

520

Give yourself a hug. Say, "You're a heckuva person," and mean it.

521

Designate "Pamper Day" with your mate. Take turns. One day a month one of you does whatever the other one desires, however preposterous the request.

522

Walk up to a kindly stranger; ask for his or her autograph.

523

Put a bird feeder outside your bedroom window.

524

Start a collection of the weirdest headlines from checkout counter tabloids.

525

Go for a moonlight swim in the buff with a friend.

526

Make your own worry beads.

527

Smile slightly while under verbal attack.

528

Drive to work with a "Just Married" sign on the back of your car. Look sheepish.

529

Don't interrupt the person you love, ever.

530

Play "Doctor" with your lover.

531

Have breakfast with your imaginary "guardian angel." Tell him/her all the wonderful things you're going to accomplish this week.

532

Write to world leaders. Invite them to dinner at your house next time they're in the country. Don't be surprised if they come a-knockin'. It's the kind of PR that tempts the new global consciousness.

533

Spend some time in a hayloft with your lover.

534

Ask your mate how you can be more romantic.
Surprise him or her soon after.

535

Go Christmas caroling with a mariachi band.

536

Tip someone for serving someone else.

537

Put a sign on the front lawn of a friend:
FREE DONKEY RIDES; INQUIRE WITHIN.

538

Locate the town of your ancestors. Learn all you can about it. Visit it one day.

539

Sponsor a humorous speech contest in your local high school. Get a local merchant to donate a prize. Be a judge.

540

Gate-crash a lawn party of blue bloods. Use the words *panache, auteur,* and *déjà vu* often, and they'll never suspect you.

541

Hire a 300-pound biker to be your bodyguard
for a day.

542

Be the first to hold an authentic garage sale.
Put up a sign. Then try to sell your garage!

543

Rent a video camera. Put it on a tripod.
Turn it on and interview yourself on
what a great life you're having.

544

Go with your significant other to a lively nightspot—separately. Try to pick each other up.

545

Use "opening-line grabbers." Don't just say hello on the phone. Grab people's attention with a fun statement, for example: "So, how do you want the $6.4 million you just won in the state lottery? In monthly installments or all at once?"

546

Send a telegram to your lover.

547

Put up a humor bulletin board at work. Start it going by displaying cartoons and appropriate wacky articles. It'll catch on quickly.

548

Interview yourself as if you were on a T.V. talk show hyping a book on your life.

549

Send yourself a balloon bouquet on the toughest day of the year.

550

Arrange to change jobs with someone in your company for one day. Call it a "Moccasin Program"—I walk in your moccasins, you walk in mine. You'll wind up appreciating each other a whole lot more, not to mention have some fun doing something different.

551

Buy a pair of knickers. Go play miniature golf.

552

Go jump in a lake.

553

Do a tap dance on the steps of city hall.

554

Talk friendly to your vital organs.

555

Buy a large, plastic, inflatable world globe. Sit on it frequently. Sing "I'm Sitting on Top of the World." If you're still breathing and you've got your health, then you are.

WE'D LIKE TO HEAR YOUR (HAPPY) THOUGHTS

We'd like you to tell us what brightens <u>your</u> day. Whether it's loony or tame, funny or far-out, if you have an idea or two that lightens the load or makes you laugh out loud, let us know what they are and we may use them in an upcoming collection of ways to put more fun in your life. Send your suggestions to the attention of The Fun Motivator, c/o The Globe Pequot Press at the address below.

ORDER THIS BOOK at a discount
for your friends, business associates, social group or club

For special discounts see your local bookseller,
or call toll-free 24 hours a day 1-800-243-0495 (in Connecticut,
call 1-800-962-0973) or write to

The Globe Pequot Press
P.O. Box 833
Old Saybrook
Connecticut, 06475-0833.

Also, for information on special discounts for corporate or other large group sales, please contact John Chamberlain, Special Sales Manager, The Globe Pequot Press.